Hot and Cold

Sally Hewitt

CHILDREN'S PRESS®

A Di   shing

NEW YO   SYDNEY

DANBURY, CONNECTICUT

Acknowledgments:
Bruce Coleman p. 8tr (Robert Maier);
Robert Harding p. 23b (Patrick Matthews), 27t;
Image Bank pp. 8tl (Doug Sundberg), 9l (David de Lossy), 14bl (T. Anderson),
25r (Michael Salas); Milepost 92 1/2 pp. 15l, 26l (Colin Garratt);
Oxford Scientific Films p. 22t (Geoff Kidd), 24br (Anna Walsh); The Stock Market p. 26r.
Thanks, too, to our models: Luke Jackson-Abeson, Fay Beaman, Conor Pavitt,
James Moller, Naomi Ramplin, Shaheen Amirhosseini, Gemma Suleyman.

Series editor: Rachel Cooke
Designer: Mo Choy
Consultant: Sally Nankivell-Aston
Photography: Ray Moller unless otherwise acknowledged

First published in 1999 by Franklin Watts
96 Leonard Street, London EC2A 4XD

First American edition 2000 by Children's Press
A division of Grolier Publishing
90 Sherman Turnpike, Danbury, CT 06816

Visit Children's Press on the Internet at:
http://publishing.grolier.com

A CIP catalog record for this book is
available from the Library of Congress

ISBN 0-516-21654-6

Contents

Hot and Cold

You can tell whether things are hot or cold by how they feel. Often you don't even have to touch them. You can feel heat coming from very hot things and cold coming from very cold things. You must always be very careful.

A fire can make you feel warm and cozy, but if you get too close, it will burn you.

The sun can make you feel nice and warm, but on a hot day it could burn your skin, so you need to wear a hat and put on sunblock.

Test the bathwater before you get in to make sure it is not too hot.

THINK ABOUT IT!

You can feel if something is hot. How else might you be able to tell if something was very hot?

Things feel hot or cold because of heat. Cold things have less heat than hot things.

A can of soda feels cold when you take it out of the refrigerator.

Eating ice cream makes your mouth feel cold.

TRY IT OUT!

Make lists of things that feel hot, warm, and cold. Draw pictures of them as well.

7

Heat

The sun gives our planet Earth all its heat and light.
Nothing could live without heat **energy** from the sun.

Plants use energy from the sun to grow.   Many animals eat plants for energy.

Plants and animals give
us the food we eat.
Food gives you the
energy you need to
make heat. Your
body makes heat
all the time.

Animals' bodies make heat, too. A cat feels very warm to cuddle.

Feel where a cat or dog has just been lying.

Heat from its body has made the place warm.

 ## THINK ABOUT IT!

Does your bed feel warm or cold when you climb into it at night? How does it feel when you wake up in the morning? Can you say why?

 ## TRY IT OUT!

Take two coins from a purse. They feel very cold. Hold one coin in your hand for a few minutes and leave the other on a table. Now put them on the inside of your wrist and feel them both again. Can you feel how heat from your body has warmed up the coin you held?

9

Just Right

Sara is neither hot nor cold. She is feeling just right!

Do you think she would still feel just right if she wrapped herself up in the thick woolly blanket?

How do you think she might feel if someone opened a window and let cold air into the room?

Which clothes would Sara put on to keep warm outside on a cold day? What would she put on to keep cool outside on a hot day?

💡 **THINK ABOUT IT!**

Do you feel most comfortable when you are hot, cold, or warm?

10

When you have been running around and working hard, you get very hot. Your body makes drops of water called **sweat**. Sweat helps cool you down.

Do you sometimes **shiver** when you get very cold? The tiny movements your body makes when you shiver help warm you up.

Which of these things would help cool you down?
Which would warm you up?

What else can you think of that would warm you up?
What else would cool you down?

11

Temperature

We measure how hot or cold things are by taking their **temperature** with a thermometer. Temperature is measured in degrees Fahrenheit and Centigrade, marked on the **thermometer**.

You can take the temperature of all kinds of things, including the air, water, and your own body.

When you are not very well and have a fever, you feel either too hot or freezing cold!

 TRY IT OUT!

Ask an adult to help you take your temperature. A normal temperature is 98.6°F (37°C.)

LOOK AGAIN

Look again at page 11 to find what else can make you feel too hot or too cold.

When you bake a cake, you set the oven temperature using a dial on the front of the oven.

THINK ABOUT IT!

Why do you need to know the temperature inside an oven when you are baking? What could happen if you didn't know?

You can set the temperature on a central-heating system. The heat will turn on when it gets too cold and off when it gets too hot.

What else do you need to know the temperature for?

Changes with Heat

When things are heated, they can change. They may change shape or look different in other ways.
Water heated so hot that it bubbles and boils turns into a **gas** called **steam**.

Some **solid** things like metal and plastic **melt** and become a **liquid** when they are very hot. When they cool down they become solid again.

Paper and wood catch fire when they become very hot.

As things become hotter they usually get bigger. We say they **expand**.
When a metal lid on a jar gets stuck, run it under hot water. The metal lid gets hotter and expands. It is easy to twist off.

 THINK ABOUT IT!

Railway lines are placed with room for them to expand.
What do you think would make them get bigger and then smaller again?

When things are cooled down, they usually become smaller. They can get harder and more brittle, too.

 TRY IT OUT!

Put some modeling clay in the refrigerator to cool it.
Take it out — how does it feel? Is it easy to use?
Warm it with the heat from your hands.
Is it easy to use now?
What difference do you notice?

Freezing Cold

Chilling or freezing food helps keep it fresh. Germs that make food go bad cannot grow in very cold temperatures.

 TRY IT OUT!

Find two pieces of cheese and two slices of bread and four plastic food bags. Put a slice of bread or a piece of cheese into each bag and seal them up.

Put two bags on the windowsill, one with cheese and one with bread. Put the other two in the refrigerator. Check them each day. What do you notice? Why do you think food in the refrigerator stays fresh longer?

Most food needs to be kept in a cool place. Do you think there is any food that needs to be kept in a hot place?

The inside of a refrigerator feels cold, but the outside feels warm. This is because the tube at the back of the refrigerator takes heat away from the inside and lets it out into the air.

 SAFETY WARNING

Never touch the back of a refrigerator.

Water that is chilled to 32°F (0°C) **freezes** into **ice**. We use the freezer compartment of a refrigerator to make ice and freeze food. Frozen food keeps for a long time.

Mammoths have been found frozen in ice. They have been there for 10,000 years. This helps us know what a mammoth looked like, even though they are now extinct.

17

Hot Food

Raw food changes in all kinds of different ways when it is cooked.

Sometimes we add baking powder to flour when we mix up a cake.
The powder makes little gas bubbles in the mixture.
Heat from the oven makes the little bubbles
expand so the mixture rises.

There is a little pocket of gas inside
an egg. Boiling the egg makes
the gas expand. Sometimes
it bursts the shell open!

How does a raw egg
look different from a
fried egg?

Butter, chocolate, and cheese all melt when they are heated.

👁 LOOK AGAIN

Look again at pages 14 and 15. What else melts when heated? What other things expand when they are heated?

✋ TRY IT OUT!

Grate cheese onto some toast. Ask an adult to put it under a broiler. Carefully, watch the cheese bubble and melt in the heat. Let it cool and cut it into strips for a snack.

In what ways has cooking changed all these things?

19

Moving Heat

You often start to feel cold when you get up and push off your blankets or comforter. Heat escapes from your warm body into the colder air of your bedroom.

A bathrobe and slippers will help stop the heat from escaping.

Inside a room, most objects are the same temperature as the air around them. We call this **room temperature**. A hot pie taken from the oven slowly cools down to room temperature.

 TRY IT OUT!

Fill one mug with hot water and another with chilled water. Leave both mugs on the kitchen table overnight. In the morning, test the temperature of the water in each mug with your finger. Is the water the same temperature in both mugs? What do you think has happened?

Heat on the move travels more easily through some things than others.

Heat travels easily through metal. A metal frying pan gets very hot and helps cook the food. Heat does not travel easily through wood, so a wooden handle will not get hot and burn your hand.

Heat does not move quickly through the thick foam of this cooler. It keeps your picnic lunch cool on a warm, sunny day.

💡 THINK ABOUT IT!

Do you think a cooler would stop heat from escaping from hot food, too, if you wanted a hot meal?

Warming Up

Rays from the sun heat Earth. The rays travel in straight lines; they cannot go around or through objects, so they cast a **shadow**. It is darker and cooler in the shade.

☀ TRY IT OUT!

Put some objects like these in the sun and leave them for about half an hour. Feel them. How hot are they? Which is the hottest?

Put them in the shade and feel them after about 10 minutes. Are they still warm? Have they cooled down?

A hot radiator can heat up a whole room. Hot air moves around and around, so you don't have to stand next to the radiator to keep warm.

A radiator heats the air around it. The warm air becomes lighter and rises. Cold air moves to take its place. It is heated by the radiator and rises up, too.

THINK ABOUT IT!

What can you do to keep the warm air in a room from escaping?

Sun rays shine through glass and heat the air inside a greenhouse.
The warm air is trapped inside. Plants that like the heat grow in the warmth.

Making Heat

Heat is made when things rub together.

 TRY IT OUT!

When your hands are cold, rub them together quickly. You will soon feel them heat up.

People used to light fires by rubbing sticks together until they were hot enough to make a spark. It took a very long time!

Chemicals in the head of a match burst into flame after just one strike against the side of the match box.

Fire can only burn when there is a gas called oxygen. Oxygen is part of the air. Firefighters use foam to put out some fires. It stops oxygen in the air from getting to the fire, so the fire goes out.

We call things we burn to give us heat **fuel**. Wood is a kind of fuel. You can see wood burning on the bonfire on the opposite page. Natural gas is burned to give heat for cooking.

 SAFETY WARNING

Don't play with matches. Fire is dangerous. You can burn too!

LOOK AGAIN

Look again at page 14. How does wood change when you burn it? What happens to its color and shape?

Energy

Heat is a kind of energy. We use heat to make things work.

Coal fires on old trains heat water to make steam. Steam is used to drive the **engines** that power the train.

Gasoline is the fuel a car engine burns to give the car the energy to move.

 LOOK AGAIN

Look again at page 8 to find what kind of fuel your body needs to make heat and to give you the energy you need to grow and move.

Electricity is a kind of energy made in power stations. It can be made by burning natural gas, oil, or coal to heat water to make steam. Steam turns blades called **turbines** around and around very fast. Turbines power machines called **generators** that make electricity.

Electricity flows along cables to our homes.

Electricity heats the flat bottom of an iron.

Electricity turns on the television.

Electricity makes lights shine. The lightbulb gets hot, so don't touch it!

THINK ABOUT IT!

What would happen if there was a power outage and there was no electricity? How many things in your home would still work? What could you use to keep warm or to light up the dark without electricity?

27

Useful Words

Electricity Electricity is a kind of energy that can be made in power stations. We use it to power televisions and all kinds of other machines.

Energy Energy is what people, animals, and machines need to give them the power to do work. Energy comes in different forms such as heat and electricity. It can change from one form to another.

Engine Machines such as cars and airplanes have engines. An engine is the part of a machine that gives it the power it needs to work.

Expand To expand means to spread out or to get bigger. Things usually expand when they get hot.

Freeze When water becomes colder than 32°F (0°C), it changes into solid ice. We say it freezes.

Fuel Coal, gas, and oil are all kinds of fuel. They are burned to make energy. Gasoline is another fuel made from oil.

Gas The air all around us is made up of a mixture of different gases. Gas does not have a shape of its own.

Generator A generator is a kind of machine that makes electricity.

Ice When liquid water is cooled below 32°F (0°C), it freezes into solid ice.

Liquid Water, oil, and juice are all liquids. A liquid can be poured and does not have a shape of its own.

Melt When a solid is heated and turns into a liquid, we say it melts. When solid ice becomes warm, it melts into liquid water.

Room temperature Room temperature is the temperature of air inside a room.

Shadow A shadow is a patch of darkness made when light cannot shine through a solid object.

Shiver You shiver when you get very cold. Your body makes lots of tiny movements that make heat energy to warm you up.

Solid Solid things like ice and wood are neither liquid nor gas. They have a shape of their own.

Steam When water is heated, it boils and turns into a hot gas called steam.

Sweat When you get very hot, your body gives out drops of water through your skin called sweat. Sweating helps you cool down.

Temperature The temperature of something is how hot or cold it is. We measure temperature in degrees Fahrenheit (°F) or Centigrade (°C) using a thermometer.

Thermometer We use a thermometer to measure temperature.

Turbines Turbines are blades that spin very fast when water, gas, or steam rushes over them. Spinning turbines in a generator make electricity.

Index

About This Book

Children are natural scientists. They learn by touching and feeling, noticing, asking questions, and trying things out for themselves. The books in the *It's Science!* series are designed for the way children learn. Familiar objects are used as starting points for further learning. *Hot and Cold* starts with the hot and cold things we encounter each day and explores heat and its effects.

Each double page spread introduces a new topic, such as the temperature. Information is given, questions asked, and activities suggested that encourage children to make discoveries and develop new ideas for themselves.
Look for these panels throughout the book:

TRY IT OUT! indicates a simple activity, using safe materials, that proves or explores a point.
THINK ABOUT IT! indicates a question inspired by the information on the page but that points the reader to areas not covered by the book.
LOOK AGAIN introduces a cross-referencing activity that links themes and facts through the book.

Encourage children not to take the familiar world for granted. Point things out, ask questions, and enjoy making scientific discoveries together.